W9-BTF-559

THE WORLD OF AUTOMOBILES

Customizing Your Ride

Written by Norm Geddis

The World of Automobiles

Carmakers from Around the Globe

Concept Cars: Past and Future

Customizing Your Ride

Hop Inside the Most Exotic Cars

Toughest Trucks From the Streets to Showtime

THE WORLD OF AUTOMOBILES

Customizing Your Ride

Written by Norm Geddis

MASON CREST

Mason Crest
450 Parkway Drive, Suite D
Broomall, Pennsylvania 19008
(866) MCP-BOOK (toll free)

Copyright © 2019 by Mason Crest, an imprint of National Highlights, Inc. All rights reserved. No part of this publication may be reproduced or transmitted in any form or by any means, electronic or mechanical, including photocopying, recording, taping, or any information storage and retrieval system, without permission from the publisher.

First printing
9 8 7 6 5 4 3 2 1

ISBN (hardback) 978-1-4222-4089-2
ISBN (series) 978-1-4222-4086-1
ISBN (ebook) 978-1-4222-7708-9

Library of Congress Cataloging-in-Publication Data

    Names: Geddis, Norm, author.
    Title: Customizing your ride / Norm Geddis.
    Description: Broomall, Pennsylvania : Mason Crest, [2019] | Series: The world
       of automobiles.
    Identifiers: LCCN 2018018047 (print) | LCCN 2018018422 (ebook) | ISBN
       9781422277089 (eBook) | ISBN 9781422240892 (hardback) | ISBN
       9781422240861 (series)
    Subjects: LCSH: Automobiles--Customizing.
    Classification: LCC TL255.2 (ebook) | LCC TL255.2 .G43 2019 (print) | DDC
       629.28/7--dc23
    LC record available at https://lccn.loc.gov/2018018047

Developed and Produced by National Highlights Inc.
Editor: Andrew Luke
Interior and cover design: Annalisa Gumbrecht, Studio Gumbrecht
Production: Michelle Luke

QR CODES AND LINKS TO THIRD-PARTY CONTENT

You may gain access to certain third-party content ("Third-Party Sites") by scanning and using the QR Codes that appear in this publication (the "QR Codes"). We do not operate or control in any respect any information, products, or services on such Third-Party Sites linked to by us via the QR Codes included in this publication, and we assume no responsibility for any materials you may access using the QR Codes. Your use of the QR Codes may be subject to terms, limitations, or restrictions set forth in the applicable terms of use or otherwise established by the owners of the Third-Party Sites. Our linking to such Third-Party Sites via the QR Codes does not imply an endorsement or sponsorship of such Third-Party Sites or the information, products, or services offered on or through the Third-Party Sites, nor does it imply an endorsement or sponsorship of this publication by the owners of such Third-Party Sites.

CONTENTS

KEY ICONS TO LOOK FOR:

Words to understand: These words with their easy-to-understand definitions will increase the reader's understanding of the text while building vocabulary skills.

Sidebars: This boxed material within the main text allows readers to build knowledge, gain insights, explore possibilities, and broaden their perspectives by weaving together additional information to provide realistic and holistic perspectives.

Educational videos. Readers can view videos by scanning our QR codes, providing them with additional educational content to supplement the text. Examples include news coverage, moments in history, speeches, iconic sports moments, and much more!

Text-dependent questions: These questions send the reader back to the text for more careful attention to the evidence presented there.

Research projects: Readers are pointed toward areas of further inquiry connected to each chapter. Suggestions are provided for projects that encourage deeper research and analysis.

Series of glossary of key terms: This back-of-the-book glossary contains terminology used throughout this series. Words found here increase the reader's ability to read and comprehend higher-level books and articles in this field.

WORDS TO UNDERSTAND

aftermarket
a secondary market available after sales in the original market are finished

chassis
a frame upon which the main parts of an automobile are built

horseless carriage
the original phrase used to describe what would become known as the automobile

Model As and Ts
the most famous early Ford model cars

CHAPTER 1

You Bought It, Do What You Want With It

For some people, deciding which car to buy is only the first step in owning an automobile. Since the early days of **Model As and Ts** a unique culture has flourished among owners who seek added speed and style, creating stand-out vehicles that make personal statements. Why should a production model stock car have to stay just a bland stock car? Once it's bought and paid for, the owner may do what he or she likes. And many owners do just that!

The statements that owners make come in two varieties. First are the owners who announce their arrival with neon lights,

Car customization has existed since the early days of the Ford Model T.

booming sound systems, and an extravagant paint job. Another favorite, along with the flash of a customized body, is the roar of a supercharged engine bursting from a stock car body that will also turn heads. Often a custom car will sport both wild engine upgrades and wild accessories whose only purpose is to turn heads.

These customized road creatures say something about the period in which they were created. Even when the Model As and Ts were new on the market, there existed custom parts and even custom options from Ford. That may come as a surprise. Founder Henry Ford once said about the Models A and T that customers could have the car in any color they liked, as long as it was black (the truth is that the Model T came in red and blue as well in its first few years of production). He wasn't into giving customers choices. But customer demand led to the quick evolution of what's called the auto parts' **aftermarket**, and Ford wasn't going to be left behind.

The Ford Model A, like this 1929 Tudor, was intended to be a class above the Model T.

The Ford Model A was made in two series. The first Model As were built between 1903–1904 and were open two seaters. The 'A' stood for 'Advanced,' as in the Ford Advanced Automobile. The later Model A was a classier upgrade from the Model T. It had a wide, enclosed cab and leather coats. The Model T (for Tin Lizzie) was Ford's first car for the masses. Reliable and easy to maintain, the Model T was an enclosed four-seater that was the first car to sell over one million units. These cars provided choice bodies to break apart and weld into mechanical monsters.

Today the automobile aftermarket approaches one hundred fifty billion dollars in sales annually, and the market is growing by 2.5% per year. About 16.4 million cars are sold in the United States each year. That's just production models from Ford, Honda, Toyota, GM, and other carmakers. Each person who buys a car also buys some kind of accessory. Maybe it is something no flashier than car mats that gets added to a new car, but just about every new car owner gets something to individualize their new set of wheels.

LEGAL TRICKS

The US government passed a law in 1975 protecting the right to "trick out a ride" without worry. The law is called The Magnuson-Moss Warranty Act. It makes it illegal for car makers to void a car's warranty simply for using aftermarket parts. This means that if a Ford owner decides to switch out exhaust systems then Ford cannot say they will no longer honor the car's warranty on the remaining parts.

In this book, the extreme examples of customization will be

In the 1970s, racing stripes like the ones on this 1970 Oldsmobile Cutlass were a common custom addition.

explored, not just the addition of a bobblehead or two. These cars will be ones that defy imagination and, in some cases, have literally been turned upside down.

Somewhere in the neighborhood of six generations of car owners have been using their automobiles as moving canvases. They've splashed all manner of abstract and realistic objects across them. Custom cars can often be dated by their paint jobs. Today's exotic paint jobs often appear to express complicated geometric formulas, which create illusions with angled lines, blurring the actual shape of the car. Custom cars in the 1970s often sported racing lines or even silkscreen paintings of landscapes, dragons, and attractive women. The 1960s was the era of Day-Glo colors and abstract images painted on cars. Prior to the '60s, most paint jobs served a strictly utilitarian purpose. Hot rods often got only a coat of grey or black primer.

While custom car art and body creations became recognized as an art form in the 1970s, the early days were more about getting the job done than making cars look pretty. Car customizers didn't have a great reputation either. In post-war

America, drag racing was seen as the activity of hoodlums because there were several street racing accidents involving young men and women in heavily customized cars whose tragic deaths made for attention-grabbing headlines. Then, of course, parents wanted their concerns addressed by local schools and police. Unfortunately, the more frequently tragic racing deaths happened, the more dramatic the headlines became and the more concerned parents became.

Not only were parents concerned, but car builders and drivers who loved the sport did not want to see it made into a villain. As much as anyone else, drag racers didn't want to get hurt and didn't want to hurt anyone. They did like, however, bruising egos on the race track. The pressure from the negative publicity and the legitimate concerns of parents led the big names in car customizing and drag racing to organize their sport with rules, safety requirements, and the stipulation that all racing be done on organized tracks, not streets.

But from the beginning of automobile mass production, youths were driven to deck out their cars. It took little more than a decade for the aftermarket to get a foothold, and by the 1910s, carmakers were offering their own custom options. Within the higher end car market of the time, the options were what defined the car.

The Benz motor company (later Mercedes-Benz) was the first to offer brake pads. The pads were invented during a cross-Germany tour of one of the early Benz cars. As a publicity stunt of to show off how easy the Benz automobiles were to drive, Karl Benz's wife, Bertha, put herself and their teen children in a Benz #3 model and drove to see her mother. This was a completely open vehicle, a literal horseless carriage, and the carriage was not fancy, but rather open, small, and cramped.

Driving to see mom isn't a big deal today, but at the time it constituted the first cross-country car trip of any real distance. At the time, there were no fuel stations or even a fuel industry. Bertha Benz stopped at pharmacies along the way to buy the chemicals needed to fuel the car. When the wooden brake shoes kept falling off, she stopped at a blacksmith where she designed and had the blacksmith make the first brake pads, using leather attached to iron castings, in a matter of a few hours.

If not for this trip, there may never have been a company called Mercedes-Benz. Bertha Benz took the trip without informing her husband, who suffered from debilitating anxiety and insecurity. He believed his car would never make any money. So in order to show that a car could be useful, and to encourage her husband, she made the first cross-country journey where she not only invented the brake pad but also improved elements of the car's fuel line. Newspapers around Europe got wind of Bertha's trip and by the end that drive to mom's became the most famous car journey to-date.

Not every car company was fortunate enough to have a Bertha Benz. The period beginning after 1885 and ending around the time of the First World War saw many horseless

Watch an original Benz Patent Motorwagen 1 in action from 2014. The horseless carriage shown here was made in January 1886. The commentary is in German, but you don't need words to know this is really cool!

carriage companies come and go. This was the era of the first model cars, in which automakers would make many versions of the same vehicle. While Henry Ford is credited with bringing the assembly line to auto making, it was Karl Benz who created the first series of model cars with the Benz Patent Motorwagen. Before 1885, cars were available on a limited basis in the United States. These cars were all made to order, each one unique. Often the buyer would have to makeshift a horse carriage onto the horseless part. One company would create the **chassis**. Another company would make the motor, and a third would provide the carriage. Sometimes a fourth company was needed to put the whole car together.

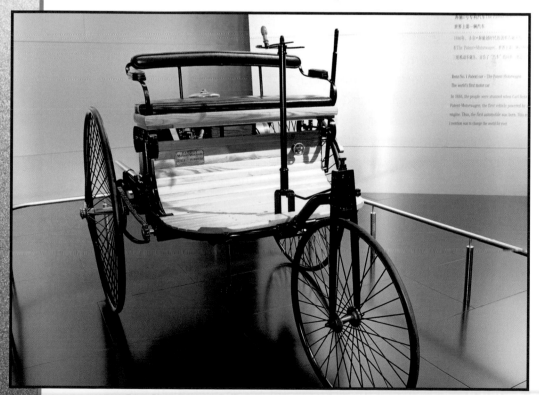

The Benz Patent Motorwagen, seen here on exhibition in China, was designed to create the first series of model cars.

Some inventions take a long time to arrive at the marketplace. The television was one of them.

The television was first demonstrated at the 1875 World's Fair in London, and it took a century before every home in America had one. Automobiles, surprisingly, were a long-expected invention. An article from an 1885 issue of the *Salt Lake City Tribune* describes the **horseless carriage** as something everyone had been waiting for, for about seventy years. The headline of the article read, "Factories for the construction of the new vehicle now springing up all over the United States. We shall soon match Europe in this matter, but it will be bad for horse breeders and farmers." The article, which appeared in various forms in many other papers around the county, touted the fact that the next year, 1886, would be the first year the horseless carriage would be available in the United States.

The first aftermarket part was arguably a headlamp and taillight set made by the Pockley Automobile Electric Lighting Syndicate in England in 1908. Their set was unique for the time in that it was for any horseless carriage and added a significant feature available on only the most expensive automobiles. And that's really the motivation for customizing a car: to give the average car some of the gravitas of the most expensive cars.

The Pockley light set came with a set of headlamps, sidelights, taillights, and an 8-volt battery, the most powerful battery for a set of car lamps at the time. The set required its own battery as cars did not yet produce enough power to light their own lamps. Even production models of the time, like the Peerless, ran their headlamps off of separate batteries.

As the twentieth century got rolling, more and more people got themselves automobiles. By the 1920s, just about every city had several auto parts stores, many selling their own

In 1885, the Salt Lake City Tribune published an article declaring that the long awaited horseless carriage would be available in the United States the following year.

parts claiming to improve performance on Fords, Buicks, and other cars. Just as car customization really got going with stories of the first drag races being held on the same day as Pearl Harbor, everything got put on hold for World War II. After the war, all the pent-up frustration of the Depression and the war exploded over American culture. Just as homes, entertainment, and even food were changing, cars and the way people interact with them changed too. The Interstate Highway System began in the 1950s and was completed in the 1970s, allowing the country to be traversed by car in about four days. The previous Federal Highway system was a patchwork of local roads and a cross-country journey took about ten days to two weeks.

CALIFORNIA NIGHTMARE

Getting to California was quite a job before the Interstate Highways System. A number of drivers lost their lives. Getting from Kingman, AZ, to California on Route 66 required a trip backward down a steep hill. That part of Route 66 is today inaccessible. A number of old crashed cars sit in the ravine below to this day, a visceral reminder of just how adventurous one had to be, even in the twentieth century, to get to California.

The completion of the Interstate Highway System in the 1970s allowed for easy cross-country travel. A coast-to-coast trip could be accomplished in four days.

1. True or False? The automobile was an invention that took everyone by surprise.

2. What was the first car accessory, or aftermarket part?

3. What was the first Model automobile?

 RESEARCH PROJECT

Go to a car show or meet. There are literally thousands of car shows and car meets around the United States. Note both the styles of yesterday and the latest styles in customization. This will give you an appreciation of just how many generations have been into customizing. The Car Show Finder website will help you find one near you: http://www.carshowfinder.org

air compressor
a device in which air at atmospheric pressure is forced into a space from which it can then be delivered at a higher pressure

entropy
a measure of the unavailable energy in a closed thermodynamic system (i.e. a combustion engine) that is also usually considered to be a measure of the system's disorder

The Second Law of Thermodynamics
the state of entropy of the entire universe, as an isolated system, will always increase over time

CHAPTER 2

Adding Power and Style

With electric cars on the rise and electric supercars expected in a few years, a whole new set of parts and processes will emerge for increasing speed. For the moment, however, the good old internal combustion engine will have to do. So, what are the best options for adding power to today's cars? The answer starts up front, at the engine's intake.

The intake manifold of a high performance engine.

Intake

Increasing airflow into a car engine increases power and speed. An automobile engine is essentially an air compressor inside an oven. Air combines with gases produced by burning fuel to turn chemical energy into mechanical energy. This occurs because the combination of gases creates extreme pressure. The pressure then turns the engine's pistons. Other options besides pistons exist and have been used in the past, but pistons run almost all cars today.

Due to the **Second Law of Thermodynamics**, a lot of leftover chemical energy turns into heat. That heat can go up and up in temperature, but can never go down as long as the engine is in operation.

Then bam! The engine blows up.

Just kidding. That would happen, except that because of The Second Law of Thermodynamics engineers can determine the exact rate of what is called entropy inside an engine. **Entropy**, generally, is a measurement of wasted energy inside a system. In this case, the wasted energy manifests itself as heat. Since engineers can design an engine to maintain its entropy rate, the engine doesn't blow up. They

When an engine overheats, it causes the pistons to stop turning, and the engine fails.

know the heat resistance of the materials and make sure the engine is cooled appropriately through the radiator system.

IGNITING PASSION

Gottlieb Daimler and Karl Benz were two of Germany's most inventive automobile engineers. However, while companies they individually founded became Mercedes-Benz, the two men never met and were said to despise each other from a distance. Years before their companies merged, they went through a long and expensive patent lawsuit over a car ignition system. Daimler won the suit in which it was determined that the early Benz ignition system came after Daimler's patent went into effect and was largely a copy of the Daimler system.

Engines do catch fire because of failures in the cooling or gasoline distribution systems. They rarely explode. Still, it's not an exaggeration to say that without solid engineering, an internal combustion engine would go BOOM!

Most often when engines overheat the pistons stop turning. This happens because of a mechanical failure that lets all the potential energy become heat—entropy again. Eventually, the heat causes a breakdown of the reaction process and all the pressure dissipates. The pistons come to a standstill. When the engine cools it will likely operate again, as long as further damages have not occurred, such as broken pieces flying around inside the engine.

Gottlieb Daimler first patented the supercharger in 1885. The design has come a long way since then.

An air intake system in today's cars requires a complex network of filters and sensors. In many cars, manifolds distribute just the right air and fuel mixture to each cylinder. But the air can be compressed even more.

Superchargers, Turbochargers, and Twinchargers.

Remember the description of an engine as an air compressor inside an oven? Well, what if a second air pump, with an independent power source, is put on top of the engine? The injection of further compressed air into the intake produces a sudden acceleration.

Three different types of air compressors are used to increase an engine's power, each with different advantages and drawbacks. A supercharger is powered by a belt drive on the engine, the same as a car's water pump. Gottlieb Daimler patented the first supercharger in 1885. He would go on to be key in the development of Daimler-Benz, which evolved into Mercedes-Benz. While Daimler died in 1900, before the merger of his and Karl Benz's car companies into Daimler-Benz, his patents were instrumental to Mercedes-Benz success almost thirty years later.

KEEP YOUR COOL

Not every hot engine gets cooled by a radiator system. One car motor used neither pumps, water, nor radiator fluid to cool an engine. The original VW Bug, made up to the early 1990s in Brazil and Mexico, used an air-cooled engine, bypassing the need for a liquid coolant.

Turbochargers combine mechanical and turbine driven chargers either in series or in parallel.

A turbocharger uses a turbine-driven system powered by the car's exhaust. Turbochargers have an advantage over superchargers. A turbocharger adds less heat to the air when it's blown into the engine than a supercharger does. The increased heat causes increased entropy. While both get a car moving, a turbocharger adds up to 30% more power than a supercharger. However, a supercharger is more responsive, kicking in faster than a turbocharger.

A twincharger has the best of both worlds: a combined mechanical and turbine-driven charger. These can be placed side-by-side or one on top of the other, in what are called parallel and series configurations.

Chargers can cost as little as $2,000 and as much as $15,000 or more if engineered and manufactured to custom specs. Installing them takes some talent and is usually done by master mechanics. Getting a twincharger installed and operating is the trickiest task of all.

Style Options

Sometimes it's not about what's under the hood. Sometimes the sheer look of the car is awe inspiring. From rims and wheels that make you look, to trucks that look like they're driving upside down, to neon-lined Lamborghinis riding like futuristic spacecraft on the highways of Tokyo, style carries at least as much weight as what's under the hood. Often, cars are about both. But one or the other can make for a supreme custom car.

Automobiles were known for their big fenders and runners during the 1930s. These huge wheel-covering runners are the hallmarks of Buicks and other cars from the time. The runners were so wide that if an extra passenger couldn't fit inside the car, they would step up on the runner and hang onto the side.

This was the first item that some car owners felt had to go. To make their cars sleek and more aerodynamic for street or sand racing, many wannabe race car drivers who couldn't build or buy their own race cars modified Buicks, Fords, and other

Chrome rims were a popular add-on in the 1970s, and have made a resurgence in today's custom aftermarket.

25

street cars. This was the beginning of customization. Once an afterthought in the automotive repair market, body shops began to take off. Not only did people want their cars modified for the race track, they wanted them modified to look cooler.

Rims and spoilers have been popular add-ons since the 1970s. Chrome was the most popular choice for rims until wars in Africa caused the price to rise and rim makers to innovate with new materials. Today, chrome is a more affordable option, and is popular alongside rims of every color, including neon lit and spinning rims. All of these innovations opened the mind of the car owners to wilder and wilder options. But before the price spike in the mid-70s, chrome was the only option any respectable customizer would consider. Anything else was too weird.

Spoiler styles have always had more leeway than rims. The term spoiler comes from the idea that the aerodynamically shaped tale will spoil bad air movement, making the driver sturdier control over the car. Whether this is true in every case is debatable, and some spoilers seem to have more to do with getting a crowd to say "Wow" than with the physics of air movement.

Imagination is the only limit for adding to, or creating from scratch, a car that turns heads. And, probably most importantly in today's world in which everyone uses social media, these cars get lots of smartphone camera clicks. Geometric paint jobs are a current trend. These are cars with lines that form angular patterns, disturbing the way people see the very shape of the car.

The possibility of car paint that changes color from something like red to blue using, for example, an app on a smartphone is not only real, it's been tested in the lab using nanotechnology based paints. However, an informal agreement exists between car companies and governments that this technology won't be further developed until social aspects have been researched. Such a device would be a boon to bank robbers, for example, if they could change the color of the getaway car with the touch of a button.

Custom AV

Don't forget the all-important sound system. By the 1970s, the top-of-the-line car sound system had an ear splitting full 8 watts. Today, some subwoofers for cars have 1,000 watts or more. A saying has been passed around for years that goes something like, "the automobile was built for the car radio, not the other way around." Music has always been important to the automobile, and the radio industry grew up along with the car. Today, a band can hold a full concert in front of a few hundred using a high-end car sound system.

In the custom audio world, it is not unusual for a sound system to be worth more than the car where it is installed.

Great sound is not the only thing customizers like to put in. This is the video age, after all. Video screens in the dashboard are a no-no (although they were all the rage in the 1970s and are still out there) as the driver should only be watching the road, but that doesn't mean everyone else in the car can't have a full HD visual experience. A popular customization is headrest-mounted 10-inch 1080p screens that can operate together or independently. The arrival of active headrest systems that respond automatically as a safety measure during a crash has made overhead monitor systems more popular. Wherever the screen is mounted, these systems have been customized to

Just because you are in your car and not your living room does not mean you cannot have a full HD entertainment experience.

include built-in gaming consoles with wireless handsets and headsets that can play DVD, Blu-Ray, or stream.

Custom car video is not just for entertainment these days. Custom shops can install rear view cameras of almost any design. These are not your standard backup cameras. This is an integrated video system that can toggle between views of not just behind the vehicle, but also blind spots and back seats as well.

Some of the weirder and wilder creations need to be examined in more detail, because this is the cutting edge of car building imagination. Here are a few dreams that became reality.

Rick Sullivan's Upside-Down Truck

Rick Sullivan runs a collision shop in Clinton, IL. One night in early 2014, he got a call to recover a pickup truck that had turned over in the snow. This gave him the idea to create one that could actually run on the road.

Some body parts come from several older Ford F-150 pickups. The drivetrain and cabin body come from a 1991 Ford Ranger. The lower portion of the upside-down truck comprises the Ford F-150 body while the upper part and seating come from the '91 Ford Ranger. The truck cost Sullivan about $6,000 in the cost of the tear-down bodies, drivetrain, and motor and about six months to build. This upside-down truck actually has four wheels along the side of the top part of the vehicle, and they spin!

People come from all around to see his upside-down truck, and Sullivan says that the pickup gets about 1,000 cellphone snaps a day. While Sullivan says he will never sell his inverted creation, he does have a very special series of vehicles in the works which he does plan to offer for sale.

Jeff Bloch's Upside Down Camaro

Jeff Bloch is a police sergeant who works for a Washington, DC-area police department. He is also an amateur race car driver and car customizer. He built an upside-down Camaro, which might be strange, but his first creation was also odd. Jeff is the man responsible for The Spirit of LeMons, an aircraft-shaped car made from an aircraft fuel tank that was designed to look like the famous aircraft The Spirit of St. Louis. That airplane was the first to cross the Atlantic, flown by Charles Lindbergh.

For his Camaro, he purchased two junked cars for under $1,500. The first car to go into the mix was a 1999 Camaro convertible that had a rotten top and mildew in the interior. After tearing out the interior, reconditioning the body, and painting it, the bottom half of a Ford Fiesta became the base of the car.

In his first race at the New Jersey Motorsport Park with the new creation, the upside-down Camaro finished in the middle of the pack. It even managed to beat a Mercedes. Even though his car didn't come in first, it did win the Grand Prize, which at this race goes to the car that does well while being ridiculous.

Wooden Custom Cars

Wood has been used in the manufacture of cars since the beginning. The first station wagons had wooden bodies because wood was less expensive than steel. This kept the family car idea of a long four-door vehicle with an extended back affordable for families to own. Come the 1970s, station wagon bodies were made of steel, save for the side panel that harkened back to the all-wood bodies. Race car makers have used wooden frames with some success. Wood is lighter than steel, allowing for better aerodynamics. But wood can break easily and if not treated, easily catches fire.

Every now and then a custom car builder gets it in his or her head to make a car out of wood. As far away as Punjab,

India, and Romania, some pretty crafty wooden cars have been constructed in small shops and garages. Weight and aerodynamic factors play a part in choosing wood as a material, but ask anyone who's made a car from wood and the reason they will likely give is that "I did it because I could."

Peter Szabo's Wooden Classic

Looking like something from the parking lot of a high-class restaurant in 1936, Peter Szabo's all-wooden body concept car is probably the largest wooden car of the last several decades. He spent three and a half years working on the car. At one point, he had to stop the project and expand the size of his garage in order to accommodate it. He made the body out of ash wood. The V6 engine comes from a 1983 Ford Taurus. Parts set Peter back about $18,000 while labor set him back another $4,500. A digital tablet was installed in the dashboard. His three-year project made a big splash at the Frankfurt Auto Show in 2015.

Early station wagons, like this late-1940s Ford model, had bodies made of wood because wood was cheaper than steel.

Peter Szabo's wooden concept car debuted at the massive Frankfurt Auto Show in 2015.

The Cardboard Lexus

That's right, a car made from cardboard, which is wood, of a sort. The Lexus replica was made out of 1,700 sheets of 10-mm-thick cardboard. The car is the brainchild of several designers and modelers in London. They took the digital schematics of a Lexus and by laser cutting the cardboard pieces were able to fashion together the car out of layers. An electric motor gives the lightweight car enough power for it to be driven on city streets. Each layer was glued together by hand. The car's seating is also made out of cardboard.

Watch as a couple of customizers take a restored Model T for a run on the Bonneville Salt Flats.

TEXT-DEPENDENT QUESTIONS

1. Why does an engine stop running when it overheats?

2. What are the differences between superchargers and turbochargers?

3. What is the principle that explains why engines heat up?

 RESEARCH PROJECT

Bonneville Salt Flats is a dry lake bed famous for annual land speed contests. Using Google Maps zoom in on the salt flats and note Interstate 80 just above the northern part of the flats. The historic name of that portion of Interstate 80 is shown on the map. Research the importance of that historic road and what it meant for the development of automobiles in the United States.

Bonneville Salt Flats

drag racer
a custom race car, usually with a long front end, that is built for racing on straightaways, with an emphasis on designing the car for maximum straight focus

master car mechanic
a certification based on education and experience that qualifies someone to work on the most unique and carefully engineered vehicles

one-off
limited to a single time, occasion, or instance

CHAPTER 3

Everything and the Kitchen Sink

Tens of thousands of dollars are spent on a car and the typical owner is most concerned with the color and sound system. Gas mileage, safety, even price get thrown out the window if a car touches the heart. That's what car designers stay awake at night worrying about—how to make a car touch the heart. For a handful of people, the heart cannot be touched unless that person gets everything they want, including the kitchen sink. In a sense, automobiles are boxes on wheels, and people like to put things in their rolling boxes and decorate them.

Lots of different kinds of people make up the world, some more outrageous than others, and some of the outrageous ones have expressed themselves in their cars with some attention-getting aftermarket parts and stylings. The aftermarket consists of an endless variety of options, from trim to turbochargers. Then there are the add-ons and cars that car creators make from scratch.

Some of the cars described below are the product of an individual's imagination, others are team projects and still others are the brainchildren of some the world's most renowned automakers.

Visitors to the 1956 Motorama car show saw a Cadillac that added to a popular expression of the time. "Everything but the kitchen sink" was a saying used to express that a product that had all the extras. Well, Cadillac took that one step further. Their custom Cadillac for the Motorama show came with its own working kitchen sink and a place for cutlery.

Dodge Deora

If upside down isn't bold enough, how about backward? Ask any custom car maker what's the oddest custom job, and the majority of them will point to the Dodge Deora, a pickup truck by Mike and Larry Alexander that has the truck bed before the cabin. The Dodge Deora wasn't just a **one-off**. It's still in production today. For at least three generations, millions of kids have been running around with one or two in their pockets. The Deora is famous in great part to the fact that Hot Wheels chose it for the first line of their diecast toys, and it's been in and out of production by Hot Wheels ever since.

Watch as a banged up 1968 Custom Camaro Hot Wheels car gets restored to factory specs.

Orbitron

The Orbitron is a bubble top 1960s futuristic **drag racer** with living room comforts and an odd history. The car body was constructed from hand-laid fiberglass, with the mechanical elements taken from several Fords, Buicks, and Chevys. Californian Ed "Big Daddy" Roth was disappointed in his creation. A cartoonist and illustrator by trade who dabbled in car customization, he felt that the car didn't show well as the body had ended up obscuring much of the chrome work he had done on the engine.

He was so disappointed that he sold the car to a friend and fellow car customizer, Darryl Starbird. Starbird was a big influence on *Star Wars* creator George Lucas, who created a fictional car by him for his film *American Graffiti*. That car was called the Superfleck Moonbird. That car has become a reality over time. One of Starbird's creations, the Predicta, is today known as the Superfleck Moonbird.

The fully restored Orbitron on display in California in 2009.

Starbird traded the Orbitron to a collector some years later. From there it made its way to Mexico, where legend says it has been seen from time to time at a carnival sideshow. By the mid-90s, the car was thought to be lost.

When the Orbitron turned up in 2007 in a parking lot as an advertisement for a local business in Juarez, Mexico, it was missing its hood and some interior parts.

The bubble top had been destroyed in the early 1970s when it became stuck. The driver was trapped inside and the plastic had to be cut to let him out.

The car has been fully restored by Ed "Newt" Newton, who assisted Roth in the original Orbitron's creation.

One of many unique features of the Orbitron is the lighting system. Three lights sit in a horn-shaped compartment on the front of the Orbitron, a red, green, and blue light. The beams are angled to collide, producing a single beam of white light emitting from the front end.

Roth's creation originally had a television in the dash that wouldn't work today since analog television signals switched to digital in 2009. The original television was one of the objects missing when the car was found in Mexico. It has since been replaced (though not able to receive signals) by an identical General Electric television found on eBay. Another throwback in the car's stylings is the baby blue faux fur lining.

Old Crow Belly Tank

The Old Crow Speed Shop in Burbank, CA, has been used as a location in many films and television shows. Plus, it's a favorite shop of former Tonight Show host, avid car collector, and **master mechanic** Jay Leno.

It's probably due to all the Hollywood action that's gone to their heads, but in 2004, car restorer Bobby Green and his crew at Old Crow Speed Shop in Burbank, CA, built the Old Crow Belly Tank, a hot rod made out the fuel cell of an early American jet fighter from just after World War II. The engine is even older, a 1932 Ford 201-cubic-inch, 3.3L, four-cylinder motor from the short-lived Ford Model B. Racing in cars built from these aerodynamic fuel cells (that were attached to the bellies of military aircraft, thus belly tanks) was all the rage in the 1950s. Green is part of a twenty-first-century revival of building and racing belly tanks.

The folks at Old Crow took their Belly Tank for a run at the Bonneville Salt Flats during Speed Week in 2008, and have set five speed records over the years.

Reactor

Californian car designer Gene Winfield's Reactor looked like half a car that had just managed to race out of collapsing time tunnel. The other half got left behind.

The car was seen by millions of television viewers. It was Catwoman's car opposite the Batmobile in the 1960s *Batman* TV show. *Star Trek* producers also hired the Reactor to be an alien's car in the episode

Belly tank racers like this one were the hot item on the California hot rod circuit in the 1950s.

titled *"Bread and Circuses"* from March 1967. The Reactor also appeared in late '60s episodes of *Bewitched* and *Mission: Impossible*.

IAMAUTO

Car customizations are not always done as one-offs, but sometimes as the concept of a particular vision. Hip-hop artist Will.I.Am announced his intent to create a car company, IAMAUTO, in 2012. However in his

Singer/actress Eartha Kitt sitting behind the wheel of Gene Winfield's Reactor in her role as Catwoman in the 1960s TV show Batman.

eagerness to drive the car, he took the prototype out for a test spin before registering it with the California DMV. He was stopped by the LAPD and the IAMAUTO car was impounded.

While in impound, officers noticed that the IAMAUTO was actually a customized DeLorean. This publicly shamed Will.I.Am and has likely ended his quest for a car company. Though many prototypes begin as a customized version of another maker's car, Will.I.Am had said on the *Tonight Show* that his car was a fully custom-built model. In fact, it was what would be called an Alpha Prototype. The problem for Will.I.Am was not that he customized someone else's car, it's that he was not honest about the stage of development of his car. In the car-customizing and creation business, integrity is essential. People pay millions for some of these cars and deserve an honest automobile.

George Barris's Creations

The designer whose cars came into American homes on a daily basis was George Barris. A native of Sacramento, CA, he became Hollywood's favorite car creator. The first car he worked on was the Munster Koach, from the 1950s TV sitcom *The Munsters*. That car, however, was designed by Tom Daniels and fabricated by Barris. The DRAG-U-LA hot rod racer that made several appearances on the show was Barris's first full television creation. That car set the stage for what has been known as the most famous television car of all time—the Batmobile.

His was a rush job. The task of creating a Batmobile originally went to designer Dean Jeffries, who made the Monkeemobile for *The Monkees* TV show. Jeffries started transforming a 1959 Cadillac, but would not be able to get it done before filming started. So at the last minute, the producers of *Batman* gave the job to Barris. He was already working on creating a customized Lincoln at the time. He refocused that effort and the most iconic Batmobile of all time came into existence.

Cars he made for other popular shows were KITT from *Knight Rider,* The Clampett's truck from the *Beverly Hillbillies* (which sits today on display at the College of the Ozarks), and the "Striped Tomato" Torino from *Starsky and Hutch*. For those with a love of 1970s forgotten television, some of the more obscure shows that sported Barris car creations were once popular Saturday morning kid shows *The Bugaloos* and *The Banana Splits*, and the detective show *Mannix*.

Barris also designed KITT, *the car from the 1982 TV series* Knight Rider. *The car is a customized 1982 Pontiac Trans Am.*

Designer George Barris created television's original Batmobile in 1966. The car was a customized Lincoln Futura, which sold at auction in 2013 for $4.2 million.

BIRTH OF THE BATMOBILE

The 1960s *Batman* television show wasn't the first live-action *Batman* series. Before many people had televisions in their homes, movie theaters ran serials, which were weekly shows that were of fifteen to twenty minutes long that ran before the main feature. Batman had two movie serials between 1943 and 1949. Neither of these serials had a Batmobile, but Batman has been using one in the comic books since 1941. In the first serial, Batman and Robin were driven to the crime scenes in a Cadillac Series 61 convertible by their butler Alfred. By the second serial series, Alfred was gone and the car had been downgraded to a Mercury.

TEXT-DEPENDENT QUESTIONS

1. How was the Orbitron being used when it was found in Mexico?
2. Which car did George Barris build that was designed by somebody else?
3. What car was built out of parts from an old fighter jet?

RESEARCH PROJECT

Think of your favorite movies or television shows involving cars. Using IMDb or other sources, research the designers of some your favorite entertainment car creations and discover some their wilder creations, not ready for prime-time.

pompadour
a man's hairstyle in which the hair is combed into a high mound in front

roadster
an automobile with an open body that seats two and has a folding fabric top and often a luggage compartment or rumble seat in the rear

speed shop
a store that focuses on building and selling parts for custom vehicles, and often creates their own custom cars

CHAPTER 4

Remix or Restore?
Two Paths to Wow!

Back during the early years after World War II, an entire generation was learning to have fun for the first time. Think about it. The average age of a World War II soldier was around twenty-six. That meant that the Great Depression had started for many soldiers at around fifteen years old. So first no jobs and no money, and then getting shot at a continent away. After all that, this generation was ready to have fun.

The 1950s was the era for roadsters, like this Buick Wildcat II.

By the 1950s, jobs were plentiful and cars were becoming the coolest thing a person could own. Primarily in Southern California, New Jersey, and parts of the Midwest, clouds of dust and pairs of lights began appearing late after midnight on surface streets, beaches, desert flats, and in dry lake beds.

Roadsters and lakesters were two different types of hot rods that came into being during this time. Roadsters were constructed out of one or more cars, i.e. two Buicks and a Ford. Lakesters, or belly tankers, were usually made from aircraft fuel tanks, making for better aerodynamics.

More by a process of evolution than by a plan, more and more curious car buffs showed up at this nighttime, and often illegal, phenomenon. But as time went on, rules were defined and standards agreed upon. Street racing was largely replaced by professional courses for drag and track racing.

Drag racing was getting such a bad name in popular culture during the early years that many people thought of race car drivers as little more than criminals. Many people were perfectly happy with their Ford or Buick as-is, and didn't understand the racing or customizing culture. As tragic deaths were not uncommon, and newspapers headlines loudly chronicled them, it was understandable that people not involved in the culture saw it with some suspicion. These were, after all, parents whose teenage kids could be out there racing. Long before texting, many mothers and fathers sat up into the late night worrying by their telephones that their teenager had been killed or arrested.

Two organizations formed out of the public concern to set boundaries and legitimize drag racing: The National Hot Rod Association (NHRA) and the Automobile Timing Association of America.

The organizations worked with local clubs in putting on community events and increasing community involvement so

The NHRA drag racing circuit was founded in 1951 to organize and promote a sport that was illegal at the time. It now has more than forty thousand registered drivers.

that racing and racers would be seen as sports enthusiasts instead of hoodlums. Clubs became involved in community education about racing safety and worked with local police to shut down illegal racing. Official rules and standards for tracks were developed by these organizations, which led to the spread of legal racing venues.

A January 1956 issue of the *Oxnard Press Courier* in coastal California told the story of the dispersal of one hundred automobiles and their drivers late one cold evening. The racers were preparing for drag races on open roads east of Ventura, CA. While police took care of business they did seem somewhat sympathetic to the racers. Captain Howard Marsh was quoted as saying most of the juveniles were, "well behaved and decent kids," who had, "no other place to drag race." The newspaper writer had a different attitude, writing that the police captain had, "a dismaying lack of common sense and community responsibility."

As early as 1952, Fresno, CA, had been giving kids spaces to race. On the last Friday of every month, open races were held on a five-thousand-foot stretch of a local airport runway.

Some drag races ended in tragedy. An example of this comes from a Santa Rosa, CA, newspaper account from June of 1961. A drag race on the local city streets had ended in the death of the passenger of one of the cars. That car had hit an oncoming car and thrown one of the passengers out

Dragsters and hot rods are highly customized works of art, each reflecting the unique personality of its builder.

of the car onto the pavement where he died. The driver was prosecuted for the crime of manslaughter.

The sport continued to have trouble legitimizing itself until *LIFE* magazine came to the rescue. *LIFE* was the most subscribed to publication in the United States. More households had a subscription to *LIFE* than had television sets up to the late 1960s.

LIFE was a magazine that came into America's living rooms around the time of the Great Depression. Though a version of *LIFE* had existed since the late 1800s, the iconic *LIFE* of photo essay fame didn't come to life until ownership changed hands in the late 1920s. *LIFE* was the primary lens through which the typical American family saw the world. It was the magazine that brought images of World War II to family back home. It was the magazine that took the world's most famous picture of Elvis Presley. The magazine ran American culture in a way no media entity ever will again. Before radio, television and the Internet, this was the closest the world had to something like Facebook or Twitter.

In 1957, *LIFE* did a photo spread on drag racing that changed America's perception of the activity. Instead of showing pale drivers hiding in the late-night dark, the spread showed professional drivers and teams racing in broad daylight, all of them very well dressed and looking good in their **pompadours**.

Today there are still tens of thousands of drag racing enthusiasts and several thousand active race tracks.

So why do hot rods and drag racers look the way they do? Why didn't some company just start producing their own racers just like car companies make regular cars?

The reason is somewhere between a lack of demand to support a full industry and a sense of honor. It's an achievement to build the car you race. Not everyone who drives a car races a drag racer. While once one of the most popular sports in the United States, the numbers of racers needed would never support production models. Plus, it is just plain fun for racers to build it themselves.

And at the time, in the 1950s, junkyards were overflowing with old Model As and Ts ripe to be remixed into some wild racing vehicles.

In fact, a junkyard in Bell, CA, began selling speed equipment in the 1920s. Since so many buyers were coming into the yard to pick parts, why not sell a few new ones too? So the owners of the junkyard began keeping a list of the parts people most asked for and then went about designing and making better ones themselves. The junkyard eventually evolved into the first **speed shop**, Bell Auto Parts.

WHAT'S IN A NAME?

Custom cars commonly have the name of their original builder worked into them. Even when the car is sold, and another customizer adds to it, the car usually retains the name of the original creator, unless the new owner does something out of this world with the car. This would be the only time a personal name will change in the moniker of a custom car.

By the beginning of the 1970s, the 1950s seemed like centuries ago. Those days of white t-shirts, cuffed jeans, and grease had long since given way to styles and attitudes

Restored cars, like this 1931 Ford Model T, are either completed using parts from several other cars, or from a complete and intact original body.

that were meant to be more modern. But not so fast. By the mid-70s movies like George Lucas's *American Graffiti* and television shows like *Happy Days* brought the 1950s back with a supercharged roar. Movies like *Grease* added to the mystique and long respected magazines like *Hot Rod* pronounced the 1950 hot rod style an art form.

Star Wars creator George Lucas is also the creator of not so famous sci-fi fantasy films, like *Willow*. *American Graffiti* is nothing like his other films. He created his second-most-successful film franchise after fellow director Francis Ford Coppola bet Lucas he couldn't write a film that would appeal to a typical audience of the time.

Side by side with the re-emergence of 1950s hot-rod styles, those Model As and Ts, Buicks, and other old cars were becoming scarce in the junkyards. As those cars were leaving the junkyards, not much new was coming in. Since the war years saw a massive decrease in the number of cars being made, junkyards became a wasteland devoid of good material. Then some of the classic cars from the post-war years started showing up. That is when interest turned from welding cars together to restoring them to their former glory. This led to new interest in fully restored models of older cars.

Car restoration is a tricky subject. Just what constitutes a restored car? For example, a Model T can be restored using parts of a frame from several Model T cars. Custom sheet-metal work can be done where original body parts cannot be found. Or, a Model T can be restored from a complete, intact body.

The most meticulous restorer can almost never find every original part from every original year of a particular automobile make or model. Compromise is the name of the car restoration game. Even when an entire antique or classic car has been found, untouched by human hands, it's still been touched by time. A car cannot sit for long without being driven. After just a couple of months hoses, belts and tires will dry out, parts will deteriorate, and unless the car has been kept secure indoors, critters will have housed themselves in the undercarriage or interior of the car. Plus, there are the effects of the elements. Wind and rain will destroy a paint job at the very least.

eBay has been the car restorer's best friend ever since it came to life in the mid-90s. But still, a dial from another radio here and a substituted water pump with similar specifications from a different model there, finding the parts is more about finding what is closest to the original, rather than insisting on the original itself.

Watch McPherson College students assemble a restored Ford Model T in mere minutes.

The price difference is astounding. A restored Model T from various chopped bodies and some custom bodywork will sell for around $15,000. A Model T restored from a full and original body will sell for four times as much at around $75,000.

Some of the most expensive cars ever sold are restoration jobs. One of the few privately owned 1954 Mercedes-Benz W196 Silver Arrow racers recently sold for $29.6 million. Thirteen others are known to exist, with six of them owned by Mercedes-Benz, three owned by museums and the other four in private collections.

There are very few Mercedes-Benz W196 Silver Arrow racers that have been fully restored. In 2013, a Silver Arrow driven by 1950s Argentine racing legend Juan Manuel Fangio sold for $31 million.

TEXT-DEPENDENT QUESTIONS

1. True or False? A lakester is a race car that runs on water.

2. What do restored cars with the highest market value have in common?

3. What is typically used in naming a custom car?

 RESEARCH PROJECT

California had some of the first race tracks in the United States. Choose and profile five of these tracks still in use today, explaining what made you choose each one.

headlight covers
an ornamentation that goes around a car's front lamp housing to draw attention to the car's lights

hood ornament
an object, usually the symbol of the carmaker, which is affixed prominently on the front center of a vehicle

Whitewalls
a tire on a car that has a white band near the rim of the wheel

CHAPTER 5

Lowriders and Hip-Hop Rides

In a similar way that 1950s style came back in the 1970s, the garish '70s style of decked out large four-door sedans with outrageous sound systems returned to the mainstream just as hip-hop was going from dangerous musical subculture to the top of the music and movie charts.

A hip-hop ride is usually a four-door or two-door luxury model vehicle that has been outfitted with extra power, an attention-getting interior, and a loud sound system. Favorites of the 1990s hip-hop era were '70s or early '80s Cadillacs, Lincolns, and Buicks. While the original style of these cars was meant to evoke danger and a gangster image, much

Chevy Impalas are popular customization targets in the hip-hop community.

of that had been traded for a love of 1970s funk and disco music and the styles that went with it.

These cars have weird **headlight covers**, big **hood ornaments**, and a wild paint job. Today, aftermarket companies sell kits to turn a luxury sedan into a hip-hop ride.

IMPALA IDOLS

The Chevy Impala is a popular hip-hop ride. Snoop Dogg, T-Pain, and Rick Ross all own or owned tricked out Chevy Impalas.

Conversions include round, enlarged headlight covers, or covers in another weird shape. Chrome hubcaps with flywheels and other ornaments of their own, plus wide **whitewalls** are part of the wheels of any respectable hip-hop ride package. Vinyl tops and velour interiors are also favorites. Inside, there might be a mounted television, a siren, extra instrumentation mounted on the dash, and whatever else the imagination conjures.

Brown Sugar and Sticky Icky

Rapper Snoop Dogg has a car collection to rival a lower-level sultan's. He counts several top-of-the-line Mercedes, Rolls Royces, and other supercars in his collection. But as his car collection's manager, Big Slice, says Snoop's favorites are the cars "that are from when we're from. We always dreamin' when we get older that's what we want."

Watch as Snoop Dogg gives a tour of his favorite hip-hop ride.

Not only does Snoop own several lowrider Cadillacs, but Big Slice has turned them into unique creations each with their own name. He has two Fleetwoods, one a 1969 model that he calls the Brown Sugar and the other he calls Sticky Icky. Brown Sugar is emblazoned with Snoop Dogg's name across the front of the hood. Inside, this car's roof sports a chandelier.

Sticky Icky is painted green with a mural of Snoop Dogg outside his house with his other cars. A toy version of the car was the top-selling, 1:16-scale model car at Walmart.

Snoop Dogg gave Kobe Bryant one of his prized cars as a gift for the pro basketball player's retirement. In 1964 the Los Angeles Lakers made it to the NBA finals only to fall in a dramatic loss to the Boston Celtics. This started a rivalry between the Lakers and Celtics that would last for decades. That year's Laker team holds a special place in

Rap icon Snoop Dogg has several top-of-the-line Mercedes, Rolls Royces, and other supercars in his extensive automobile collection.

Snoop Dogg's heart. Long before Kobe Bryant's retirement, Snoop Dogg had Big Slice create the Laker '64, a Laker yellow 1964 Chevy Impala. On the front hood are images of Snoop Dogg in a Laker uniform along with famous Lakers like Wilt Chamberlin.

Cars have been a part of hip-hop since its earliest days in the Bronx, NY. Artists like Grandmaster Flash and Afrika Bambaataa wrote about owning Lincolns and Cadillacs in what are considered some of the earliest original rap songs. Hip-hop music reflects life on the streets, and Cadillacs were the choice car in Harlem, Brooklyn, and the Bronx in the heyday of disco. While young kids were inventing a new type of music, they were dreaming this music would carry them to the high life they saw around them. Little did they know it would get some of them much, much further.

After the unthinkable happened and hip-hop artists made money that made rock stars look like they were making middle-class livings, their car goals changed along with their incomes.

NWA was probably the first West Coast rap group that made it big nationally. By then, artists like Run-D.M.C. and Public Enemy had shown that hip-hop could top the charts. What had seemed like a dream in the mid-1970s to Bronx founders looked like a possibility to artists like NWA's Dr. Dre, who in one song called for donations to his Ferrari fund.

Snoop Dogg gave ex-NBA superstar Kobe Bryant a tricked out 1964 Impala as a retirement gift in 2016.

As artists grew older and began families, their songs talked about Cadillac Escalades and their kids' college funds. Today, the social car climbing isn't letting up. Maybachs and Bugatti's occupy the minds of Jay-Z and other top musicians of the 2010s.

VILLIAN VEHICLE

George Barris, the creator of the Batmobile, made a hip-hop ride for use by the bad guys in the James Bond movie *Live and Let Die*.

In the 1990s, rappers like Tupac Shakur turned SUV's, in his case a Hummer, into hip-hop rides. By the time MTV had a show about hip-hop rides in the early 2000s, the large luxury sedans were left to retirees and every other kind of car was decked out on the show, even a Ford Focus.

Thirty years ago, rapper Dr. Dre wrote about needing a fund to get himself a new Ferrari. Today, the songwriter, producer, and businessman is worth about $830 million, or enough to buy more than three thousand five hundred Ferraris.

A highly customized Ford Focus on display at a car show in Russia in 2017.

TEXT-DEPENDENT QUESTIONS

1. True or False? Snoop Dogg has a chandelier hanging from the roof of one his hip-hop rides

2. What SUV did Tupac have transformed into his hip-hop ride?

3. What are the favorite cars hip-hop artists love to turn into rides?

 RESEARCH PROJECT

Make a list of your five favorite musical artists. Chances are they are successful and rich. See if you can find out which cars they own today, and which cars they owned before they were famous.

Asia-Pacific

Asian countries and regions bordering the Pacific Ocean

askance

with suspicion, mistrust, or disapproval

Kustom Kulture

an isolated term used specifically by car customizers to reference the style and culture of the custom car industry, its fans, buyers, sellers, and artists

CHAPTER 6

Today's Car Culture: Old School Adopts High Tech

The **Asia-Pacific** area has the largest and most robust **Kustom Kulture** outside of the United States, with the most popular car shows and meets happening in Malaysia and Japan. In fact, Malaysia holds the world's largest annual car and motorcycle show, Art of Speed. The event showcases both custom cars and motorcycles, along with tattoos, t-shirts, and other art related to the scene.

The 2017 Art of Speed event even sported a skate park courtesy of House of Vans.

The Art of Speed event in Malaysia is the world's largest annual car and motorcycle show.

Hot Wheels' lead designer Jun Imai was a featured guest at the 2017 event. He discussed how Hot Wheels decides which car creations get to have diecast pocket toys made of them. Surprisingly, the silhouette of a car is the most important consideration for Hot Wheels. The company seeks to have a wide variety of cars in each new lineup, so no two vehicles should have the same basic profile shape.

Next, Hot Wheels takes into account the popularity of a car. Winners of Best in Show go to the front of the line, which means winners at Art of Speed will likely become Hot Wheels creations unless they are very similar to another planned Hot Wheels car.

Hot Wheels itself is the product of new and old custom culture. Matchbox cars made a splash on the toy market in the 1950s. Other competitors came and went, but none could knock Matchbox off its throne until someone got the idea of making diecast toy cars of the wildest and most imaginative creations. Matchbox concentrated on making toys of the cars mom and dad bought. Hot Wheel created the cars seen in an older brother's Hot Rod magazine. Add to this the fast spinning wheels and the famous orange track and a product was born that not only gave Matchbox a run for its money but eventually sold more toys than Matchbox.

HOT WHEELS

Harry Bentley Bradley, a member of the team that created the real-life Dodge Deora, designed eleven of the original Hot Wheels vehicles.

One of the most popular cars in the show was a creation by Japanese designer Daisuke Sakon of Kustomstyle in Yokohama. His custom 1949 Ford "shoebox" with gold flames on a gold-painted body was an attention getter, but it was a Mercedes replica that won Best in Show.

The "shoebox" Ford is a nickname for the 1949 Custom Fordor Sedan (Ford's spelling). This was the first new post-World War II car from any of America's big three automakers (Ford, GM, and Chrysler). During the war, auto plants were prohibited from doing any non-war work without permission from the US government. Few new cars were made during those years or the years immediately after the war. What cars were made were based on models from before the war.

The Fordor got its "shoebox" nickname from the car's slab-like look, and it's most famous feature is its curved front windshield. This style of car was known by engineers of the

The Ford Fordor sedan was the first new post-WWII car from any of the big three U.S. automakers.

time as the "pontoon" look. The shoebox or pontoon look began a style of car shape that's still with us today.

Kustomstyle gave their Ford a dark gold paint job with lighter gold flames shooting over the full length of the car, including on the roof and trunk

A replica Mercedes won Best in Show at a major car show event because it's a replica of one of the most sought-after cars for mechanical customization.

Watch this report on a neon happy custom supercar crew in Japan.

The owner of the winning Mercedes at Art of Speed likes his anonymity, but his mid-90s Mercedes W201 Evolution replica was turning heads at local races before it showed up at Art of Speed. Now that it won Best in Show he'll have a harder time keeping his identity a secret. Following the 2017 show, however, still no one claims to know who made it, and the maker isn't speaking up either. The car is a mystery.

Winners of Best in Show in both the Motorcycle and Car divisions go to the MOONEYES Yokohama Hotrod Custom Show as Guests of Honor.

The Mercedes W201 was Mercedes's first attempt at a smaller, less expensive car. It turned out to be a favorite among stock car racers. It was a smallish four-door sedan labeled an "executive compact." For reasons that have to do with ease of getting under the hood and taking things apart, this car also became a customizing legend. This led Mercedes to come out with their own power version of the W201, the Evolution.

So sought after are real versions of the Evolution, that had the Art of Speed winning automobile been a real Evolution, the owner would likely never take it out on the street. An original stock Evolution sells for over a quarter of a million dollars, challenging the price of some of today's most expensive new Mercedes, like an AMG.

The greatest thing about today's custom culture is that it's open to all styles. For people who didn't grow up between the 1950s and the end of the twentieth century, it can be

The Mercedes W201 Evolution is one of the most sought-after cars for customization. Only 502 were produced in 1990. The car had impressive top-end power capabilities due to a redesigned engine with a higher rev limit due to its shorter stroke and bigger bore.

difficult to understand just how rigid American culture was about style. The wrong thing at the wrong time would receive a fair amount of ridicule. A hot rod made from two Buicks and a Ford at a late 1960s meet would have been looked at **askance**. Muscle cars were the rage of the late 1960s. They were marketed to young adults and the price tag wasn't anything like today. A Ford Mustang was sold at the time by the same edict with which Henry Ford introduced the Model T. Henry Ford was quoted in the early 1900s as saying, "No man making a good salary will be unable to own one [a Ford motor car]."

But leave that Ford Mustang alone? Not likely. An early 1970s car meet would see a parking lot lined with customized Ford Mustangs along with Plymouth GTXs, Dodge Chargers,

Cars like this 1970 Ford Mustang 302 Boss were prime targets for customization in the 1970s.

maybe even an Australian Holden, or a Ford Falcon Cobra. An old 1950s Hot Rod would have been a throwback.

Fashion worked along a strict linear path in the twentieth century. What was "out of style" was never supposed to come back. What changed that was information. Information, first in the form of magazines and clubs, made it ok to go back. Once Hot Rod magazine declared the 1950s *Hot Rod* style an art form, and clubs in one city heard of hot rod styles coming back in another, suddenly expressing the past became acceptable.

The cast of the TV show Mad Men *at the 2009 Emmy Awards Show. Don Draper, a character in the show played by John Hamm (center), described nostalgia as "a twinge in your heart far more powerful than memory alone."*

By the 2000s, the Internet was instrumental in dissolving those styles, and expressing and mixing old styles not only became acceptable but the very definition of cool.

It first started in the late 1970s, when nostalgia gave styles from prior decades a new life. Nostalgia is an emotion that was possibly best described in *Mad Men*, a fictional TV show about advertising. Don Draper, a character in the show, described nostalgia as, "a twinge in your heart far more powerful than memory alone." Writer Milan Kundera wrote that nostalgia is the "irrepressible yearning to return," and, "the power of the past."

Even young people experience it, the yearning to return to younger age, even if just a few years ago by number. But because of experience, hormones, and maturity, that period of time can never be completely regained. It's a feeling all humans experience from time to time. One of the only known remedies is to touch something from that past, to hold it and feel it. Young people are lucky in this regard. Many have keepsake boxes or the spaces in the backs of closets for such things. Adults, for the most part, let those things go for one reason or another over their own lifetimes. They must resort to eBay.

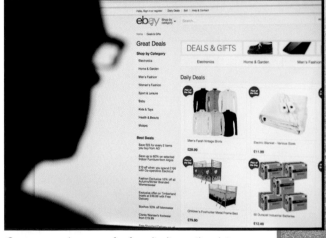

Grown ups who yearn for favorite items they let go of over the years can feed their nostalgia through popular auction website eBay.

1. Why are some Mercedes from the 1980s so sought after for conversion into race cars today?

2. True or False? The United States holds the largest car show in the world.

3. Which model represented Mercedes' first attempt at a smaller, less expensive car?

 RESEARCH PROJECT

Get to know an artist. No, seriously. Find a car customizing artist in your area (no matter where you are there's likely to be at least one) and interview him or her about what makes the culture special.

Series Glossary of Key Terms

Aerodynamic Drag

Drag produced by a moving object as it displaces the air in its path. Aerodynamic drag is a force usually measured in pounds; it increases in proportion to the object's frontal area, its drag coefficient, and the square of its speed.

Ball Joint

A flexible joint consisting of a ball in a socket, used primarily in front suspensions because it can accommodate a wide range of angular motion.

Camshaft

A shaft fitted with several cams, whose lobes push on valve lifters to convert rotary motion into linear motion. One or more camshafts regulate the opening and closing of the valves in all piston engines.

Carbon Fiber

Threadlike strands of pure carbon that are extremely strong in tension (that is, when pulled) and are reasonably flexible. Carbon fiber can be bound in a matrix of plastic resin by heat, vacuum, or pressure to form a composite that is strong and light—and very expensive.

Chassis

A general term that refers to all of the mechanical parts of a car attached to a structural frame. In cars with unitized construction, the chassis comprises everything but the body of the car.

Cylinder

The round, straight-sided cavity in which the pistons move up and down. Typically made of cast iron and formed as a part of the block.

Differential

A special gearbox designed so that the torque fed into it is split and delivered to two outputs that can turn at different speeds. Differentials within axles are designed to split torque evenly; however, when used between the front and rear axles in four-wheel-drive systems (a center differential), they can be designed to apportion torque unevenly.

Drivetrain

All of a car's components that create power and transmit it to the wheels; i.e. the engine, the transmission, the differential(s), the hubs, and any interconnecting shafts.

Fuel Injection

Any system that meters fuel to an engine by measuring its needs and then regulating the fuel flow, by electronic or mechanical means, through a pump and injectors. Throttle-body injection locates the injector(s) centrally in the throttle-body housing, while port injection allocates at least one injector for each cylinder near its intake port.

Horsepower

The common unit of measurement of an engine's power. One horsepower equals 550 foot-pounds per second, the power needed to lift 550 pounds one foot off the ground in one second: or one pound 550 feet up in the same time.

Intake Manifold

The network of passages that direct air or air-fuel mixture from the throttle body to the intake ports in the cylinder head. The flow typically proceeds from the throttle body into a chamber called the plenum, which in turn feeds individual tubes, called runners, leading to each intake port. Engine breathing is enhanced if the intake manifold is configured to optimize the pressure pulses in the intake system.

Overdrive

Any gearset in which the output shaft turns faster than the input shaft. Overdrive gears are used in most modern transmissions because they reduce engine rpm and improve fuel economy.

Overhead Cam

The type of valvetrain arrangement in which the engine's camshaft(s) is in its cylinder head(s). When the camshaft(s) is placed close to the valves, the valvetrain components can be stiffer and lighter, allowing the valves to open and close more rapidly and the engine to run at higher rpm. In a single-overhead-cam (SOHC) layout, one camshaft actuates all of the valves in a cylinder head. In a double-overhead-camshaft (DOHC) layout, one camshaft actuates the intake valves, and one camshaft operates the exhaust valves.

Powertrain

An engine and transmission combination.

Rack-and-Pinion

A steering mechanism that consists of a gear in mesh with a toothed bar, called a ""rack."" The ends of the rack are linked to the steered wheels with tie rods. When the steering shaft rotates the gear, it moves the rack from side to side: turning the wheels.

Sedan

As used by *Car and Driver*, the term "sedan" refers to a fixed-roof car with at least four doors or any fixed-roof two-door car with at least 33 cubic feet of rear interior volume, according to measurements based on SAE standard J1100.

Shock Absorber

A device that converts motion into heat, usually by forcing oil through small internal passages in a tubular housing. Used primarily to dampen suspension oscillations, shock absorbers respond to motion.

Spoiler

An aerodynamic device that changes the direction of airflow in order to reduce lift or aerodynamic drag and/or improve engine cooling.

Supercharger

An air compressor used to force more air into an engine than it can inhale on its own. The term is frequently applied only to mechanically driven compressors, but it actually encompasses all varieties of compressors.

Turbocharger

A supercharger powered by an exhaust-driven turbine. Turbochargers always use centrifugal-flow compressors, which operate efficiently at the high rotational speeds produced by the exhaust turbine.

Source: caranddriver.com

FURTHER READING

Funk, Maximilian. *The Drive: Custom Cars and Their Builders*. Germany: Gestalten, 2016.

Lawrence, Tim (Mr. Fireball). *Fireball Tim's Custom Car Coloring Book: Color The Cool.* Charleston: Createspace, 2016.

Mayes, Alan. *Custom Cars: Coupes, Sedans, Pickups*. Osceola: Motorbooks, 2010.

McCollum, Sean. *Custom Cars: The Ins and Outs of Tuners, Hot Rods, and Other Muscle Cars.* Mankato: Capstone, 2010.

INTERNET RESOURCES

http://www.jalopyjournal.com/
Website for news about what's going on car restoration. Includes a forum for discussion of old cars and hot rods.

http://www.ckdeluxe.com/
Online magazine focusing on the hot rod end of Kar Kulture.

http://www.nhra.com/nhra
Official site of the governing body of professional drag racing.

http://jalopnik.com/
Website about everything to do with things on wheels, going back thousands of years.

http://time.com/3680877/hot-rods/
Drag racing photos from the LIFE magazine archive.

http://www.infinitegarage.com/late-1950s-drag-racing-footage/
Vintage drag-racing footage primarily from home movies.

EDUCATIONAL VIDEO LINKS:

Chapter 1:

http://x-qr.net/1GYL

Chapter 4:

http://x-qr.net/1Eci

Chapter 2:

http://x-qr.net/1Efz

Chapter 5:

http://x-qr.net/1FmW

Chapter 3:

http://x-qr.net/1G3f

Chapter 6:

http://x-qr.net/1FRQ

PHOTO CREDITS:

Cover Photos
ID 191812 © Rodolfo Arpia | Dreamstime
ID 11754969 © Calyx22 | Dreamstime
ID 22338020 © Michael Ludwig | Dreamstime
ID 33228372 © Oceanlau | Dreamstime
ID 42271455 © Shuo Wang | Dreamstime
ID 49523890 © Anton Matveev | Dreamstime
ID 53618433 © CarolRobert | Dreamstime
ID 60332700 © Haiyin | Dreamstime
ID 70387183 © Ben White | Dreamstime

Chapter 1
ID 35036158 © Alexmax | Dreamstime
ID 7418534 © Raytags | Dreamstime
ID 19933805 © James Boardman | Dreamstime
ID 67530939 © Steve Lagreca | Dreamstime
ID 22129890 © Jianhua Liang | Dreamstime
ID 24868819 © Saltcityphotography | Dreamstime
ID 50443372 © Carolyn Franks | Dreamstime

Chapter 2
ID 4216523 © Lbarn | Dreamstime
ID 15010350 © Otto Dusbaba | Dreamstime
ID 90627417 © Edoardo Nicolino | Dreamstime
ID 13746208 © Steve Mann | Dreamstime
ID 89371403 © Sombat Khanthongdi | Dreamstime
ID 104216768 © Jason Finn | Dreamstime
ID 10363585 © Goce Risteski | Dreamstime
ID 41538570 © Shuo Wang | Dreamstime.com
ID 50945237 © Mark Roger Bailey | Dreamstime
ID 96476923 © VanderWolfImages | Dreamstime

Chapter 3
ID 7555237 © Dana Kenneth Johnson | Dreamstime
http://flickr.com/photos/photography_nut/3222694602/
Credit – Jerry Thompson | Flickr
ID 37780447 © Redwood8 | Dreamstime
Eartha_Kitt_Catwoman_Batman_1967
https://commons.wikimedia.org/wiki/File:Eartha_Kitt_

Catwoman_Batman_1967.JPG
ABC Television | Wikipedia Commons
ID 24871443 © Carrienelson1 | Dreamstime
ID 55111152 © Selcuk Kuzu | Dreamstime

Chapter 4
ID 2932996 © Jeff Downcs | Dreamstime
ID 49486502 © Richard Gunion | Dreamstime
ID 60459300 © Joshua Rainey | Dreamstime
ID 9353674 © Hellem | Dreamstime
ID 99471336 © Fiskness | Dreamstime
Mercedes_Silver_Arrow_W196_F-1
https://commons.wikimedia.org/wiki/File:L%27evoluzione_
dell%27automobile_Mercedes_Silver_Arrow_W196_F-1.jpg
Tomislav Medak | Wikipedia Commons
ID 548543 © Tõnis Valing | Dreamstime

Chapter 5
ID 43087804 © Mattiaph | Dreamstime
ID 45927058 © Raytags | Dreamstime
ID 77991337 © Starstock | Dreamstime
D 32585373 © Sbukley | Dreamstime
ID 30571558 © Carrienelson1 | Dreamstime
ID 94270921 © Oleg Kovalenko | Dreamstime

Chapter 6
ID 44268929 © Mediagia | Dreamstime
ID 55975468 © Mohamad Ridzuan Abdul Rashid |
Dreamstime
ID 96972162 © Ryan Fletcher | Dreamstime
MercedesBenzW201_190_E_2.5-16_
Evolution_II https://commons.wikimedia.org/wiki/
File:MercedesBenzW201_190_E_2.5-16_Evolution_II.jpg
User3204 | Wikipedia Commons
ID 94209685 © Raytags | Dreamstime
ID 38021909 © Carrienelson1 | Dreamstime
ID 60581656 © Anthony Brown | Dreamstime
ID 665933 © Jorge M Vargas Jr | Dreamstime

INDEX

INDEX

INDEX

AUTHOR'S BIOGRAPHY

Norm Geddis lives in Southern California where he works as a writer, video editor, and collectibles expert. He once spent two years cataloging and appraising over one million old movie props. He is currently restoring film and video content from the 1950's DuMont Television Network for the Days of DuMont channel on Roku.